GIRLS LIKE YOU

FEATURED IN THE NETFLIX SERIES
BRIDGERTON

ORIGINALLY RECORDED BY
MAROON 5

WORDS AND MUSIC BY
ADAM LEVINE, BRITTANY HAZZARD, JASON EVIGAN, GIAN STONE AND HENRY WALTER

AS ARRANGED BY KATHY McMILLEN FOR
VITAMIN STRING QUARTET

ISBN 978-1-7051-3467-2

VSQ®
Vitamin String Quartet

DISTRIBUTED BY
HAL•LEONARD®

No part of this publication may be reproduced in any form or by
any means without the prior written permission of the Publisher.

Visit Hal Leonard Online at
www.halleonard.com

Contact us:
Hal Leonard
7777 West Bluemound Road
Milwaukee, WI 53213
Email: info@halleonard.com

In Europe, contact:
Hal Leonard Europe Limited
42 Wigmore Street
Marylebone, London, W1U 2RN
Email: info@halleonardeurope.com

In Australia, contact:
Hal Leonard Australia Pty. Ltd.
4 Lentara Court
Cheltenham, Victoria, 3192 Australia
Email: info@halleonard.com.au

GIRLS LIKE YOU

Words and Music by
Adam Levine, Brittany Hazzard,
Jason Evigan, Gian Stone and Henry Walter
As arranged by Kathy McMillen
for Vitamin String Quartet

Copyright © 2017 Songs Of Universal, Inc., Sudgee 2 Music, These Are Songs Of Pulse, People Over Planes,
BMG Platinum Songs, Bad Robot, BMG Gold Songs, Cirkut Breaker LLC and Prescription Songs
This arrangement Copyright © 2018 Songs Of Universal, Inc., Sudgee 2 Music, These Are Songs Of Pulse, People Over Planes,
BMG Platinum Songs, Bad Robot, BMG Gold Songs, Cirkut Breaker LLC and Prescription Songs
All Rights for Sudgee 2 Music Administered by Songs Of Universal, Inc.
All Rights for These Are Songs Of Pulse and People Over Planes Administered by Concord Sounds c/o Concord Music Publishing
All Rights for BMG Platinum Songs, Bad Robot and BMG Gold Songs Administered by BMG Rights Management (US) LLC
All Rights for Cirkut Breaker LLC and Prescription Songs Administered Worldwide by Kobalt Songs Music Publishing
All Rights Reserved   Used by Permission

GIRLS LIKE YOU

FEATURED IN THE NETFLIX SERIES
BRIDGERTON

ORIGINALLY RECORDED BY
MAROON 5

WORDS AND MUSIC BY
ADAM LEVINE, BRITTANY HAZZARD, JASON EVIGAN, GIAN STONE AND HENRY WALTER

AS ARRANGED BY KATHY MCMILLEN FOR
VITAMIN STRING QUARTET

ISBN 978-1-7051-3467-2

VSQ®
Vitamin String Quartet

DISTRIBUTED BY

HAL•LEONARD®

No part of this publication may be reproduced in any form or by
any means without the prior written permission of the Publisher.

Visit Hal Leonard Online at
www.halleonard.com

Contact us:
Hal Leonard
7777 West Bluemound Road
Milwaukee, WI 53213
Email: info@halleonard.com

In Europe, contact:
Hal Leonard Europe Limited
42 Wigmore Street
Marylebone, London, W1U 2RN
Email: info@halleonardeurope.com

In Australia, contact:
Hal Leonard Australia Pty. Ltd.
4 Lentara Court
Cheltenham, Victoria, 3192 Australia
Email: info@halleonard.com.au

GIRLS LIKE YOU

Words and Music by
Adam Levine, Brittany Hazzard,
Jason Evigan, Gian Stone and Henry Walter
As arranged by Kathy McMillen
for Vitamin String Quartet

Copyright © 2017 Songs Of Universal, Inc., Sudgee 2 Music, These Are Songs Of Pulse, People Over Planes,
BMG Platinum Songs, Bad Robot, BMG Gold Songs, Cirkut Breaker LLC and Prescription Songs
This arrangement Copyright © 2018 Songs Of Universal, Inc., Sudgee 2 Music, These Are Songs Of Pulse, People Over Planes,
BMG Platinum Songs, Bad Robot, BMG Gold Songs, Cirkut Breaker LLC and Prescription Songs
All Rights for Sudgee 2 Music Administered by Songs Of Universal, Inc.
All Rights for These Are Songs Of Pulse and People Over Planes Administered by Concord Sounds c/o Concord Music Publishing
All Rights for BMG Platinum Songs, Bad Robot and BMG Gold Songs Administered by BMG Rights Management (US) LLC
All Rights for Cirkut Breaker LLC and Prescription Songs Administered Worldwide by Kobalt Songs Music Publishing
All Rights Reserved   Used by Permission

41

normale

45 *p*   *mf*

53

57

61   *f*

65   *f*

69 *mf*   *f*

73 *mf*   *f*

77 *pp*

3

81 *mf* 3 3 3 3 3 3 3

86 *f*

90

94 *f*

98

sul tasto

102 *mp*   *pp*

4

GIRLS LIKE YOU

FEATURED IN THE NETFLIX SERIES
BRIDGERTON

ORIGINALLY RECORDED BY
MAROON 5

WORDS AND MUSIC BY
ADAM LEVINE, BRITTANY HAZZARD, JASON EVIGAN, GIAN STONE AND HENRY WALTER

AS ARRANGED BY KATHY MCMILLEN FOR
VITAMIN STRING QUARTET

ISBN 978-1-7051-3467-2

VSQ
Vitamin String Quartet

DISTRIBUTED BY

HAL•LEONARD®

No part of this publication may be reproduced in any form or by
any means without the prior written permission of the Publisher.

Visit Hal Leonard Online at
www.halleonard.com

Contact us:
Hal Leonard
7777 West Bluemound Road
Milwaukee, WI 53213
Email: info@halleonard.com

In Europe, contact:
Hal Leonard Europe Limited
42 Wigmore Street
Marylebone, London, W1U 2RN
Email: info@halleonardeurope.com

In Australia, contact:
Hal Leonard Australia Pty. Ltd.
4 Lentara Court
Cheltenham, Victoria, 3192 Australia
Email: info@halleonard.com.au

GIRLS LIKE YOU

Words and Music by
Adam Levine, Brittany Hazzard,
Jason Evigan, Gian Stone and Henry Walter
As arranged by Kathy McMillen
for Vitamin String Quartet

Copyright © 2017 Songs Of Universal, Inc., Sudgee 2 Music, These Are Songs Of Pulse, People Over Planes,
BMG Platinum Songs, Bad Robot, BMG Gold Songs, Cirkut Breaker LLC and Prescription Songs
This arrangement Copyright © 2018 Songs Of Universal, Inc., Sudgee 2 Music, These Are Songs Of Pulse, People Over Planes,
BMG Platinum Songs, Bad Robot, BMG Gold Songs, Cirkut Breaker LLC and Prescription Songs
All Rights for Sudgee 2 Music Administered by Songs Of Universal, Inc.
All Rights for These Are Songs Of Pulse and People Over Planes Administered by Concord Sounds c/o Concord Music Publishing
All Rights for BMG Platinum Songs, Bad Robot and BMG Gold Songs Administered by BMG Rights Management (US) LLC
All Rights for Cirkut Breaker LLC and Prescription Songs Administered Worldwide by Kobalt Songs Music Publishing
All Rights Reserved   Used by Permission

4

GIRLS LIKE YOU

FEATURED IN THE NETFLIX SERIES
BRIDGERTON

⚜

ORIGINALLY RECORDED BY
MAROON 5

WORDS AND MUSIC BY
ADAM LEVINE, BRITTANY HAZZARD, JASON EVIGAN, GIAN STONE AND HENRY WALTER

AS ARRANGED BY KATHY McMILLEN FOR
VITAMIN STRING QUARTET

ISBN 978-1-7051-3467-2

Vitamin String Quartet

DISTRIBUTED BY

No part of this publication may be reproduced in any form or by
any means without the prior written permission of the Publisher.

Visit Hal Leonard Online at
www.halleonard.com

Contact us:
Hal Leonard
7777 West Bluemound Road
Milwaukee, WI 53213
Email: info@halleonard.com

In Europe, contact:
Hal Leonard Europe Limited
42 Wigmore Street
Marylebone, London, W1U 2RN
Email: info@halleonardeurope.com

In Australia, contact:
Hal Leonard Australia Pty. Ltd.
4 Lentara Court
Cheltenham, Victoria, 3192 Australia
Email: info@halleonard.com.au

GIRLS LIKE YOU

**Words and Music by
Adam Levine, Brittany Hazzard,
Jason Evigan, Gian Stone and Henry Walter
As arranged by Kathy McMillen
for Vitamin String Quartet**

Copyright © 2017 Songs Of Universal, Inc., Sudgee 2 Music, These Are Songs Of Pulse, People Over Planes,
BMG Platinum Songs, Bad Robot, BMG Gold Songs, Cirkut Breaker LLC and Prescription Songs
This arrangement Copyright © 2018 Songs Of Universal, Inc., Sudgee 2 Music, These Are Songs Of Pulse, People Over Planes,
BMG Platinum Songs, Bad Robot, BMG Gold Songs, Cirkut Breaker LLC and Prescription Songs
All Rights for Sudgee 2 Music Administered by Songs Of Universal, Inc.
All Rights for These Are Songs Of Pulse and People Over Planes Administered by Concord Sounds c/o Concord Music Publishing
All Rights for BMG Platinum Songs, Bad Robot and BMG Gold Songs Administered by BMG Rights Management (US) LLC
All Rights for Cirkut Breaker LLC and Prescription Songs Administered Worldwide by Kobalt Songs Music Publishing
All Rights Reserved   Used by Permission

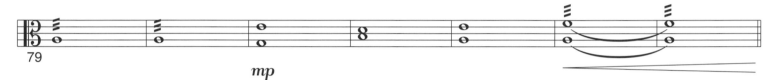

GIRLS LIKE YOU

FEATURED IN THE NETFLIX SERIES
BRIDGERTON

ORIGINALLY RECORDED BY
MAROON 5

WORDS AND MUSIC BY
ADAM LEVINE, BRITTANY HAZZARD, JASON EVIGAN, GIAN STONE AND HENRY WALTER

AS ARRANGED BY KATHY MCMILLEN FOR
VITAMIN STRING QUARTET

ISBN 978-1-7051-3467-2

Vitamin String Quartet

DISTRIBUTED BY

No part of this publication may be reproduced in any form or by any means without the prior written permission of the Publisher.

Visit Hal Leonard Online at
www.halleonard.com

Contact us:
Hal Leonard
7777 West Bluemound Road
Milwaukee, WI 53213
Email: info@halleonard.com

In Europe, contact:
Hal Leonard Europe Limited
42 Wigmore Street
Marylebone, London, W1U 2RN
Email: info@halleonardeurope.com

In Australia, contact:
Hal Leonard Australia Pty. Ltd.
4 Lentara Court
Cheltenham, Victoria, 3192 Australia
Email: info@halleonard.com.au

CELLO

GIRLS LIKE YOU

Words and Music by
Adam Levine, Brittany Hazzard,
Jason Evigan, Gian Stone and Henry Walter
As arranged by Kathy McMillen
for Vitamin String Quartet

Copyright © 2017 Songs Of Universal, Inc., Sudgee 2 Music, These Are Songs Of Pulse, People Over Planes,
BMG Platinum Songs, Bad Robot, BMG Gold Songs, Cirkut Breaker LLC and Prescription Songs
This arrangement Copyright © 2018 Songs Of Universal, Inc., Sudgee 2 Music, These Are Songs Of Pulse, People Over Planes,
BMG Platinum Songs, Bad Robot, BMG Gold Songs, Cirkut Breaker LLC and Prescription Songs
All Rights for Sudgee 2 Music Administered by Songs Of Universal, Inc.
All Rights for These Are Songs Of Pulse and People Over Planes Administered by Concord Sounds c/o Concord Music Publishing
All Rights for BMG Platinum Songs, Bad Robot and BMG Gold Songs Administered by BMG Rights Management (US) LLC
All Rights for Cirkut Breaker LLC and Prescription Songs Administered Worldwide by Kobalt Songs Music Publishing
All Rights Reserved   Used by Permission

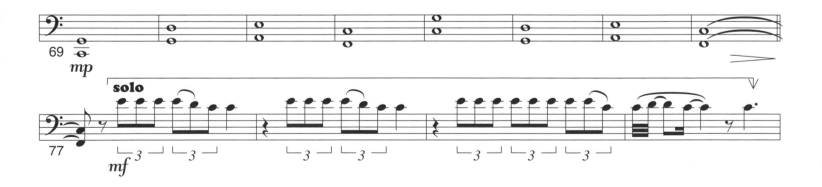

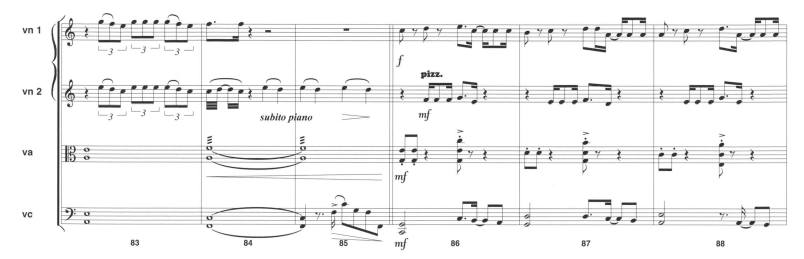